SWORDS

James Roome is a musician, poet and teacher from Manchester, UK.

Also by James Roome

The Annotated Daniel	(Steel Incisors, 2023
A crocodile, out of nowhere	(Red Ceilings Press, 2021)
Bull	(Red Ceilings Press, 2019)

CONTENTS

ISBN: 978-1-916938-34-2

The author has asserted their right to be identified as the author of this Work in accordance with the Copyright, Designs and Patents Act 1988

Cover designed by Aaron Kent

Edited and Typeset by Aaron Kent

Broken Sleep Books Ltd
PO BOX 102
Llandysul
SA44 9BG

Swords

James Roome

Broken Sleep Books

At last I must have fallen into a troubled nightmare of a doze; and slowly waking from it - half steeped in dreams - I opened my eyes, and the before sunlit room was now wrapped in outer darkness. Instantly I felt a shock running through all my frame; nothing was to be seen, and nothing was to be heard; but a supernatural hand seemed placed in mine. My arm hung over the counterpane, and the nameless, unimaginable, silent form or phantom, to which the hand belonged, seemed closely seated by my bed-side.

— Herman Melville, *Moby Dick*

THE INTERVIEW

She sat in the office waiting room, picking her nose and eating it. Her jeans were dirty. She could smell herself. A poster opposite urged her to take out a life insurance policy. She tore it down and built a fire in the wastebasket to warm her hands. The secretary remembered something he had to do, took his coat from the stand and went out. A gust of cold air whipped round the room, disturbing papers and causing the filing cabinet to fall on its side. As it fell, drawers slid open revealing reams of carefully filed papers. The ceiling fan spun into life. The light on the CCTV camera flashed. It must be summer by now, she thought. She took off her jeans and hung them over the curtain rail by the open window. Outside the office, the heat was record-breaking. Her cab driver sweltered in the taxi, engine idling. *Wait*, she'd said. *How long will you be?* he'd asked. *I don't know, just wait*, she'd said again, pressing a hand to his cheek.

SWORDS

Later, she found it. It was titled, 'The Sword'. She'd screwed it up into a tight little ball and swallowed it. It had taken a minor, self-administered surgical procedure to retrieve it from her digestive tract. As she looked at it now, partially digested, spotted with blood and stomach acid, she wondered if the party had been worth it after all.

The following day, she visited the museum where 'The Sword' was being held. On the roads, traffic slumped lethargically. She passed between the columns of the grand entrance and enquired as to the exhibition's whereabouts. When she first entered the space, she was bemused. The museum had carefully unfurled 'The Sword' and attached it, she knew not how, to a piece of wood, then hung it on the wall. There were some people standing around in silence, staring at it. Afterwards, she visited a local café and asked for a sandwich.

When the officer pulled her over, she refused to explain how it had come to be in the boot of her old Ford. She would say only: *It has been keeping me company on the long drive to the coast.* Now that she stood by the sea, in the blue shadows of mountains, she expected that it would leave. *Yes,* she admitted, *It has spilled the blood of many prominent Manhattanites.* And, *Yes, it hung above the fireplace at the family farm, and was only taken down once to slice an orange.* The officer dutifully transcribed her confessions in his notebook, as 'The Sword' crept to the lip of the boot, then fell, severing his big toe. Blood spurted from the wound. It reminded her of bolognese. The officer cried out and fell heavily to the tarmac. As the local residents arrived, she kept him talking. He groaned feebly as they carried away the toe for their children, whom it would no doubt feed for many months.

She smuggled it past the bouncers by taking it apart and secreting it beneath her coat. Later, standing in the nightclub toilets, she noticed that the blade had left a small nick on her chin. Fresh blood was dripping into the sink. Carefully, she peeled apart the edges of the wound. Something climbed out and sat, panting, on the sink's rim. The officer. She reached into her bag and took out a small wooden disc, placed the officer in the centre and sealed him in with a heavy glass dome. The dome's curved ceiling included a small air hole, but the officer had no hope of jumping that high.

She refused to surrender her bags and was taken aside by airport security. Her palms were sweaty. She knew that the contents could land her some hefty jail time. In the featureless interview room, a customs and immigration enforcement official donned plastic gloves then carefully unzipped the hold-all. He removed the head of a tiger, its fur encrusted with dried blood. He removed the arm of a chimpanzee. He placed both items carefully on the metal tabletop. He removed a terracotta leg. The customs and immigration enforcement official said nothing. He reached into the bag again and removed the officer, who seemed to be sleeping. Sleeping, or dead. The glass of his terrarium looked dirty. He had perhaps had too little light.

By the time she arrived, it was night. No-one remembered she was coming: the lights were off and the doors locked. She leaned against the car for a moment, listening to the sound of a song thrush on her phone's birdsong app. All around the car park, huge pine trees swayed in the breeze. When the valet finally turned up, he seemed flustered. She passed him the keys without meeting his eyes. He said nothing and got into the driver's seat, leaving her standing in the empty car park. She looked at the white lines of the spaces and observed that they had been repainted. There was a translation for the word, she thought, but it momentarily escaped her.

It had been three months and no-one had mentioned 'The Sword'. She ate the same breakfast every morning: scrambled eggs and brown toast. There was always someone standing in the doorway, but she could never quite catch their eye. Inside the hotel, the temperature was a constant 21 degrees celsius. The guests were all like her and the place was no worse for it. She had been forced to change rooms several times due to noise. The wallpaper was always the same. Her most recent neighbour was a retired army officer who walked with a limp. He told her stories about the war, and her own experiences paled in comparison. She did not tell him about 'The Sword', though she thought about it often. In the mornings, she would read or paint or watch a film in the basement cinema. Sometimes, the officer accompanied her. The subtitles were hard to read, but they had fun trying to make sense of them. Her own problems weren't as apparent to her then. She discovered that the officer's leg was missing below the knee, but that didn't stop him from coming along on her daily walks. The woods by the hotel were fine and unusually quiet. Occasionally, they would come to a clearing and she would remark upon the distant, blue mountains, then they would clear some moss from a rock before sitting down. It was always at this point that the officer chose to remove his prosthesis.

When she was finally released, she was unsure of what to do with herself. She remembered films in which prisoners were released after long stretches inside and were greeted by relatives or former associates who leaned against old, beat-up cars in bleak, post-industrial landscapes. There was none of that for her. Her room let out directly onto a sunlit beach at midday. She was completely unprepared. The staff had not thought to provide her with an adequate swimming costume, let alone a bucket and spade.

When she woke the next morning, ice had formed on the inside of the windows. She touched it, gently, with her fingertips. At the water's edge, she felt calm. She reached into the hold-all and pulled out a sword, threw it as far as she could. It bobbed in the swell of oncoming waves. Jellyfish swarmed to it.

She decided to stay in the city. In the city, you could get anything. Loose change. Old bedsheets. Every night, she ate in one of her favourite restaurants. *I'll have the soup!* Afterwards, she would walk down to the harbour and watch the lights of boats moving above the water. In tense moments, such as the night she saw a dog falling from a third storey window, she held herself tightly, licking her lips, muttering incoherently about oranges or spaghetti or some such. Years later, she would reflect: *How happy I was in those listless months, slouching before the TV, allowing colours to escape through an open window, gradually forgetting my form and the process of living.*

It was 8PM when the taxi pulled up outside a house she knew wasn't hers. She tried to unlock the door anyway, testing each key methodically. When she finally got inside, the hallway was crammed with laughing faces. Someone offered her wine, but she touched her stomach anxiously. As she moved through the house, the weather turned cool and dark and the walls became crowded with photographs. She paused to study them more carefully. Each one was of a different cave's interior.

The chase led her across vast deserts, into submersibles traversing unimaginably deep oceanic chasms, past cold rooms lit only by flickering candles, before eventually ending in a gym. She found it, crouching by the dumbbells, salivating over a half-eaten protein bar. *Ah ha!* she cried. Hastily, the phantom shrugged off its activewear, revealing a rippling torso, prominent veins, straining tendons. She drew a sword from the hold-all and adopted a battle stance.

The fight was intense. Several gym-goers were accidentally disembowelled, whilst others cancelled their memberships on the spot. After half an hour of uninterrupted bloodshed, a truce was declared and they retired to the changing rooms. As she sat panting on the hard wooden bench, towelling sweat from her brow, she couldn't help but stare at its face. Its appearance reminded her: it would soon be autumn; this year, she really must purchase a leaf-blower.

THE AUDITION

They arrived at the audition with nothing but the clothes on their backs. It would be a long wait, they were told. But, come on, they'd known that when they'd agreed to the meeting. They sat down together on the musty sofa and fumbled in their satchels. Both removed scripts for unshot movies. One was tea-stained. The other, torn at the corner. They began to read:

Jackie. This is your last chance.

I can't live without you.

Fog lifts over the river...

They clasp hands and stare meaningfully into each other's eyes...

...3...

Female actors should cry at this point.

...2...

Bruce. You have to believe me...

...1...

Faces resolute...

Shot rings out. Cut to birds, disturbed from the surface of a lake...

Where had they been, just before this? The director's assistant wanted to know. He looked at their damp trousers distastefully, being immaculately turned out himself. They couldn't remember, or didn't care. *Well, they're ready for you anyway.* They entered the room.

Commiserations! A friend said later, at the bar. They stayed until it started to get light, then set off home through unexpectedly busy streets. People were pushing and shoving. Someone fell in the road and had their head squashed by a lorry. Parents shielded their children's eyes. *Don't look, darling! This will give you nightmares!* When they found a lock that fitted their key, they were relieved. *What a night!* It was time to turn in; sleep away the day. It would be bright again. Enough light for another audition, perhaps. They threw open the bedroom windows and listened carefully to the sounds of the city. *At our next audition, we will be successful,* they affirmed. *Tomorrow is another day.*

THE CHRISTENING

First, they tried a high window; a tight grip round the ankle. When this didn't work, they looked for a sea captain willing to take them on a long voyage. On their third day at sea, in the middle of the night, they crept to the stern and hoisted it over churning, black waters. They looked at each other, faces white with apprehension.

The following summer, her mother woke them with the news. They sat in the kitchen sipping scalding coffee as she outlined, *next steps.* The neighbours came round. They distributed mini-whiteboards; exhibited photos, taken on the day of its birth. *What a disgruntled little face!* People whooped. Puddles were suddenly everywhere. *A pipe must have burst!* Someone suggested. They contemplated calling the emergency plumber, but decided against it. *We'll just live with it,* she said, though neither of them could swim.

THE DUVET

It had been three days since they'd lost the end of the sellotape. They turned it over and over in their hands, studying its surface under a variety of different lights. Outside in the yard, their neighbour's fiancée doused the paving stones with anti-algae formula, until the garden birds could no longer land and were forced to migrate south a little earlier than expected. They studied the TV. There was nothing in the news. When they finally straightened their backs, a thick darkness had descended like a duvet over the trees and houses.

They left through the front door and found the local postman holding a small section of duvet aloft with both hands. He'd clearly been there a while. His yellowing face was covered in a thin sheen of sweat. His knees shook. At his feet, the post bag slumped, spilling its letters and packages over the pavement. *Need a hand?* The postman shook his head. They prodded the duvet's bosomy underside. *Goose down, feels like.* The postman nodded and sneezed. They grabbed handfuls of duvet and lifted it, allowing their bodies enough space to pass, then set off to find the local shop. Occasionally, as they moved through the darkness, they heard muffled sounds: a dog snuffling; a heavy, metallic clang; a tinny beat, as if from earphones.

When they reached the local shop, Margaret was counting out her change. They recognised her from church. Her hair was longer than they remembered, and blonde, and the thick-rimmed glasses were new, but everything else about her, from the string of pearls to the patent leather handbag, felt familiar and easy to comprehend. She pushed the coins across the counter. *That should be right.* The shopkeeper nodded, then gestured to the window. The usual view of the car park was totally obscured. The duvet was pressing itself against the glass and ballooning in through the open door. *Seen that?* Margaret grunted her acknowledgement and turned to go. They watched as she disappeared into the folds of the duvet and shook their heads, then began looking for the stationery aisle. The shopkeeper nodded, ruminatively.

When they eventually found it, the sellotape section of the shelf was empty. They stood for a moment, staring at the SORRY, OUT OF STOCK sign, touching their fingertips to the cool plastic shelf-edge, as if in disbelief. *Sod's law*, they muttered. Back at the counter, the shopkeeper had disappeared. A radio played, quietly. The windows and ceiling groaned beneath the weight of the duvet, then gave way, suddenly. It spilled into the building, soft and inevitable, and the air thickened until they could barely breathe. They mouthed words as the mounting weight gradually forced them to their knees. Products fell from shelves. A tin of beans exploded beneath the pressure. The duvet filled their ears, eyes, mouths, nostrils.

They'd lain in the darkness for hours. The officer who'd pulled them from the wreckage had seemed eerily familiar. As he'd wrapped them in shiny blankets, they'd glared at his face in partial recognition. They were just in shock, he'd said, and covered in bean juice. As the only survivors, they'd been in high demand. Several national and international news networks had clamoured for their attention. A literary agent had called about selling the rights to their story to a major publishing house. The advance was rumoured to be generous.

PHANTOM

During the journey, they'd reached for the hilt several times but had never quite clutched it, though their hands had met, jarringly, like something supernatural in the centre of a long, sleepless night.

ACKNOWLEDGEMENTS

Thank you to Anabelle and Lochlan for putting up with me and my various foibles. Thank you to Mercurius Magazine and Babel Tower Notice Board for publishing early versions of these texts and thank you to Broken Sleep Books for publishing them in their final forms. Thank you to Ian Seed for reading the manuscript and for his generous blurb, and to everyone else who has supported me in any way over the last few years. Thank you, finally, to everyone who reads this book. Keep it by your bedside. Perhaps, one night, it will reach out a hand to you.

LAY OUT YOUR UNREST

www.ingramcontent.com/pod-product-compliance
Lightning Source LLC
Chambersburg PA
CBHW051741040426
42447CB00008B/1254